Surviving Life

a practical guide

by

Janice E. Taylor

∞

Creative Locations Ltd.

First published in 2014 by Creative Locations Ltd.

Saddleworth Business Centre
Huddersfield Road
Delph
Saddleworth
OL3 5DF

E-mail: creativelocations@hotmail.co.uk
Graphic design by Adam Hegab
Editing by Adelina Pintea
Printed in the United Kingdom
ISBN: 978-1-910351-08-6

Author: Janice E. Taylor
Paintings by Janice E. Taylor
www.jet-yoga.co.uk

Front cover: *'Freedom'*
Plate 1: *'Incarnation of Wisdom'*
Plate 2: *'Findhorn Bay'*
Plate 3: *'Soul call'*
Plate 4: *'Wellbeing'*

For every book sold, the author will give a small donation to animal charities of her choice. These charities will have a specific interest in the protection, maintenance and keeping of wild animals in their natural habitats.

Look fear in the face and it will cease to trouble you
- Swami Sri Yukteswar

I dedicate this book to my older sister Gill who has always looked out for me. Thank you.

Contents

Part 3: Wellbeing

Acknowledgements

*J*ohn Knowles, who walks by my side as my friend and kept me right as I began to explore my own spiritual path.

Marilyn Heginbotham, my yoga teacher from the beginning, who has allowed these practises to work through her without attachment, giving me the opportunity to experience the transformation yoga brings on all levels.

Kath Hilton, my Reiki Master, who led me through my reiki healing and training – what a wonderful gift you gave me.

Carole Kelly, who has helped me to see with clarity through the veils, to stand back and undo the patterns for myself.

Ethna Scanell, who encouraged me to keep a spiritual diary and gently imparted her wisdom along the way like a sprinkling of confetti.

Joyce Parfitt, my art teacher, who has allowed my creativity to flow unleashed without rules, structure or study; how refreshing, how colourful, how free - just like Joyce and her paintings!

Helen Brennand, my friend, who has led me back to horses and my childhood dreams, enabling a deepening connection with the horses who have become my healers and teachers. This connection has led me back to the heart and I can never repay my gratitude to you, Helen.

Thank you to Peter Walker at Vital Film and Media Ltd. for producing the CD with great expertise and sensitivity.

To David Morison, for the beautiful array of wildlife and scenic photographs he has supplied me with. I have used these for my paintings, including "The Incarnation of Wisdom" that begins this book.

To Barbara Hegab of Creative Locations Ltd: a safe pair of hands who has overseen and gently guided the process of Surviving Life from manuscript to book, with wisdom and integrity.

Family, friends and therapists. Everyone who has been part of my life, I view you all as my teachers enabling me the opportunity to grow and develop. You all have had a part to play in the writing of this book. Thank you.

Introduction

*L*ife is a journey with many potholes, some of which feel like huge gaping chasms that need to be crossed. It takes great courage to navigate our way across without falling into the abyss never to be seen again, being lost forever!

This book isn't about my journey as such, but the practical methods I have found along the way and used to help me navigate my way out of delusion, from darkness to light, fear to love. My journey is my journey and I am still on it and still learning. Your journey is your journey. It sometimes feels as if we are alone on our journey. However, we are never truly alone, we are always loved and supported from the higher realms. We get the right support at the right time, or the right person/teacher comes along when needed.

Life is an intensive training course and we are here to learn the many lessons it throws at us. If we don't learn the lessons, then it can feel like "Groundhog Day". We go around the same circles over and over again until the penny drops and we learn that particular lesson.

It's very easy to get lost in the drama of life. Sometimes we need to step off the stage and see it for what it is. Life is meant to be fun, it is our self-delusion that is the root cause of all suffering. So, when the going gets tough and you feel like you're treading through treacle or stuck in a washing machine, as my friend says, "on rinse hold", the practical methods in this book may be of some help to you. They have been invaluable to me. Some you will know, some you may not, some may help. I have included practical step-by-step approaches and case studies to aid and support you on your own journey through life.

We have no choice but to play our part in the drama of life. But we do have a choice in how well we play our part. We are given props to support us and also temptations to mislead us. The nature of this guide is to make suggestions for staying on track. We will be discussing some of the props that I have found helpful, when to use them and how to use them. *Some of our greatest foes are also our greatest teachers in life and can create the perfect opportunity for growth.* (Marianne Williamson) *Surviving Life,* hopefully will help you recognise these tests as opportunities and a chance to build resilience.

This is a distillation of everything that I have learnt and experienced, like a tried and tested literature review. The bits that have worked for me have been crystallised and written down. Why go around the edge of an overgrown garden when you can walk straight down the middle, back home?

Practical tools

*T*he first place to start is with a selection of tools that are going to support you on your journey. Some you will use all the time and others just occasionally. You may not yet be aware of all your tools, so leave space to add more as the need arises. Some you may want to try out and see if they are useful to you. I have included my tools as an example but yours may be different as we are all individuals, each one of us is unique and special and we all have separate needs. I have also given an example of some negative ways of surviving life that ultimately do us great harm if used excessively.

Author's essential tool kit

Reading, Meditation,
Yoga, Reiki, Spiritual path,
Emotional Freedom Technique(EFT,)
Animals, Nature,
Walking, Music, Painting, Art,
Friends, Camper van

Reader's essential tool kit

Author's occasional tool kit

McTimoney chiropractor,
Bach flower remedies,
Vibromuscular Harmonization
Technique(VHT)
Holistic therapies,
Homeopathy, Holidays,
Counselling, Tai-Chi

Reader's occasional tool kit

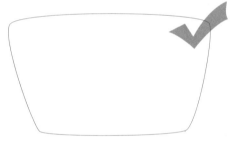

Negative, destructive coping tools that do more harm than good

Alcohol,
Television,
Drugs,
Distractions,
Cigarettes

The Health Pie Chart

We are like a wheel that requires oiling and maintaining in order for us to function effectively. I have included this as a useful tool as it helps us to see if we have a balanced healthy life and if not, what we can include in the wheel to obtain this balance.

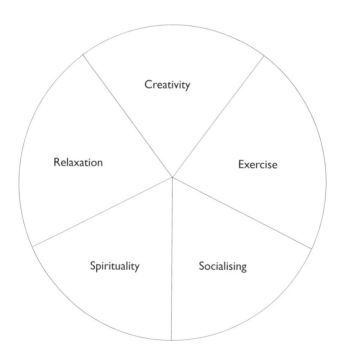

What do you do to address each of these areas in your life?
What area isn't being addressed?
What, if anything, would you like to include?

Your notes/thoughts

....
....
....
....
....
....
....
....
....
....
....
....
....
....
....
....
....
....
....
....
....
....
....
....
....
....
....
....
....
....
....
....
....
....
....
....
....

Emotions are only feelings - they are not the actual event that caused them.

Part I

Emotions

Developing love for yourself

We cannot love anyone else until we love ourselves first. Below are some ideas of how to love yourself. Some of you will find this easier to do than others.

- Be kind to yourself.
- Think of someone/something you love and give that feeling to yourself.
- Know that you are unique and special, there is only one of you.
- Believe, you are perfect just as you are.
- Tell yourself, you are loved just as you are in the higher realms.
- Use positive affirmations about yourself.
- Stand tall and proud.
- Treat yourself/pamper yourself. You deserve it.
- Look in the mirror, smile at yourself and tell yourself how lovely you are.
- Affirm "I love me" 3 times daily.
- Don't beat yourself up if you make a mistake, learn and move on.
- Treat yourself lightly/laugh/come from joy. Life is to be enjoyed.
- Achieve a work/life balance.

- Focus on positive thoughts about yourself.
- Be careful what you wish for, thoughts are powerful.
- Ask for what you would like in your life, wait and allow. See 'Ask and it is Given' (E,Hicks. J, Hicks, 2010).
- Use Emotional Freedom Technique (EFT) to tap away any negative emotions you have about yourself.

If self-esteem and confidence is a problem for you, what essential tool may help? Yoga was the tool that helped me. A saying that I found useful was Francesca's mantra:

"When things get tough, this too will pass"
"When things are good, this too will pass"

This mantra helped me appreciate the good times and the bad times while having gratitude for both.

Case study

Whilst doing Reiki for a friend who was feeling lonely after just having retired from work and feeling a little adrift with life, I heard a still voice within say to me: "you must always remember just how much you are loved". With those words, I felt an overwhelming feeling of love that lasted for days. I felt that this message is for each one of us from the higher realms. Each one of us is loved just as we are.

Stress

Modern day living can be very stressful. We can feel under constant pressure in our fast-moving world, with so many demands placed on us. Stress can also be caused by boredom or not having enough to do. Stress, however, is not always negative; we need a certain level of stress to function effectively in life. Stress can be a welcome, positive and enjoyable experience. It all depends on the demands placed upon us.

Stress affects different people in different ways at different times. How well a person copes with stress depends very much on how full their glass is with issues. If the glass is only half full then a few more issues will be manageable. If, however, the glass is full to the brim then one more problem could allow the glass to overflow and push that person over the top, even with what appears to be a relatively small problem, it maybe the final straw.

In response to stressful situations the adrenal glands in our bodies produce adrenaline and noradrenaline that prepare our body for fight or flight. This affects the blood vessels and causes the heart to beat faster, pumping more blood around the body which may cause high blood pressure, blurred vision, breathing problems and sweating. Adrenaline also affects the digestive system and the digestion becomes interrupted, the mouth becomes dry and the stomach becomes more acid, causing heart burn and nausea.The liver releases sugar for energy, muscles relax causing diarrhoea.

Feeling stressed for long periods of time without any outlet can be detrimental to our health. If we do not prevent or manage our stress levels then it can lead to long-term health conditions such as heart disease, stomach ulcers, stroke, depression, diabetes, irritable bowel syndrome to name but a few.

We can, however, help to prevent and manage our stress by developing an all-round approach to health and wellbeing. This includes a balanced diet, exercise, sufficient sleep, developing positive relationships, having a positive outlook and practising relaxation. All this helps to bring peace and harmony into our lives.

Other factors also include what support systems are in place and how a person chooses to react. This will have an influence on the function of the autonomic nervous system responsible for the release of adrenaline that ultimately determines how we feel.

I remember having acupuncture at 36 years of age, after which I experienced relaxation for the first time. I did not know this was how it felt to be relaxed as I did not know that I wasn't relaxed in the first place. I had nothing to compare it to. I had waited 36 years to experience this revelation.

Overpage is a body for you to label how you feel and think when stressed. This can be used later in the book as we progress into talking about the body's early warning system of potential danger.

Short-term effects of stress

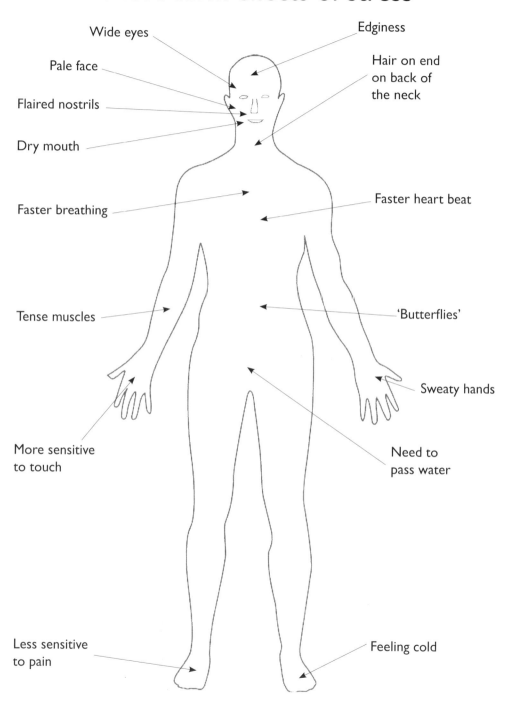

Wide eyes

Edginess

Pale face

Hair on end on back of the neck

Flaired nostrils

Dry mouth

Faster breathing

Faster heart beat

Tense muscles

'Butterflies'

Sweaty hands

More sensitive to touch

Need to pass water

Less sensitive to pain

Feeling cold

Your short-term effects of stress

(Using the diagram on the previous page, now fill in your own
symptoms of stress, on the body diagram below)

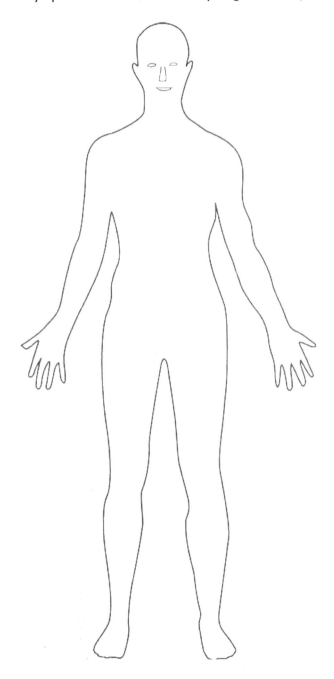

Fear and Anxiety

Anxiety, in my experience, is a collection of symptoms that alerts me to an issue or underlying problem that needs some attention that was previously masked to me and is now ready to be faced.

There are many ways to deal with anxiety. We can bury our head and pretend it doesn't exist but it tends to keep re-emerging until it's impossible to ignore any longer. This is when we can use our tool kit to help manage the symptoms but also find out what the body is trying to tell us and use the occasional tools to help us delve a little deeper, to let go once and for all. Below are some suggestions that have worked for me:

- My approach is to be in it and experience the uncomfortable feelings. Do not be tempted to distract yourself.
- Listen to what the body is telling you.
- Write down any dreams or visions and ask yourself what they mean to you.
- Use your tool kit; mine is yoga, reiki, meditation and rescue remedy.

- EFT is a self-help tool and is very useful in uncovering underlying issues and letting go of them. Sometimes accessing the memory of the cause is necessary and other times it is ok to just let go of the blocked energy in the body. Sometimes I will start by tapping on one issue and this turns into several issues, like one tree turns into a forest of issues all felled at once.
- I found counselling useful when a lot of past memories had surfaced and I needed to make sense of it all.
- Concerning deeper issues, Neuro-Linguistic Programming (NLP) was useful alongside EFT, with support from a qualified neuro-linguistic practitioner.

In "Soulcraft" Bill Plotkin talks about us having "loyal soldiers as defences" that have protected us through life. As our own confidence and personal power develops, our "loyal soldiers" no longer serve us, in fact they can hold us back. These can then be thanked and let go of, which can be an ongoing process and a long-held default position. I have sometimes noticed that I automatically fall into "sympathetic mode" or "fight and flight mode" when adrenaline is coursing through the body in an uncontrolled way. I will be unconsciously gripping my stomach.

I have now realised that this is my first line of defence, which I use alongside other alert signals within the body as an early warning system alerting me to any perceived threat from outside. I have a habit of burying my head in the sand and the higher the threat, the deeper I bury it. This may have served me well in the past and helped me to survive. Using this method of defence has obvious drawbacks for an adult living in the modern world.

I have devised my own early warning radar system as

a colour-coded, smiley-faced numbered continuum, as an example of listening to my body and using the messages to my advantage, alerting me to a problem. Then, using positive tools, I deal with the threat in a more empowered and healthier way. This example is shown later on in these pages.

The following pages include a selection of situations personally experienced when my body has alerted me to a potential problem. I have documented the methods I used to recognise them, alter the pattern, to learn the lesson and to move on. By sharing these experiences, my hope is that it will help you to recognise some of your unhelpful recurring themes. I have also included situations other people have faced with support from myself. "Your Body Speaks Your Mind" by Debbie Shapiro is a helpful book in deciphering the message from the body.

Thoughts are powerful

Thoughts are powerful, yet half the time we allow them to run off and have a mind of their own. It is useful to observe the congruency: say what you mean, mean what you think and have the body language to match. Often, these thoughts are all saying different things simultaneously which is misleading to ourselves and to others.

Thoughts are affected by our belief systems that are influenced by the environment and family we grow up in. This, in turn, affects our attitude to life and ultimately our behaviour. Ancestral patterns can play a huge part in how we think and how we act. We often hear it said that someone becomes their mother or their father even though they do not particularly want to be like them or even agree with them most of the time.

It is interesting to stand back from it all and observe your thought processes. Perhaps keep a thought dairy. Do you have a tendency to express yourself negatively or expect the worse? Is your glass half-empty? If so, this is what you will attract, based on the law of attraction ("Ask and it is Given" Esther and Gerry Hicks). People who lack confidence tend to have a negative outlook on life. (Marianne Williamson)

It is of great benefit to you and to those around you to

alter the negative self-talk into positive self-talk. You could use your thought diary and when you catch yourself in a negative thought pattern, see if you can alter it to more positive thinking, which is more likely to lead to positive outcomes. Positive thinking also helps us to have more self-confidence and self-esteem.

Worry

I have known the answer to not worrying for many years, I have read about it in several books. Branden Bays in "The Journey" talks about total surrender and letting go, even providing methods for how to go about it.

Not only do I know about letting go intellectually, but I have all my daily practices in my tool box to aid me in my letting go; yoga, meditation, reiki and EFT. People will tell you "try not to worry" - easier said than done! My friend Helen has asked me to specifically write about worry because it seems that everyone is doing it, worrying themselves sick.

I have also witnessed Helen make the shift from worrying to not worrying. How did she do it? She surrendered and let go.

As I have agreed to write something about worrying I realise that, despite all the above, I have not quite got there myself. I still haven't managed to trust enough to let go completely. In my body, I am fully aware of this.

On reflection, I wonder if it is because not worrying is not doing rather than doing; not aiming for something or attaining it. In essence, my goal is to not worry, but all I need to do in order to achieve this is to let go, to undo rather than do. The key to this is to be brave, trust and take the plunge. What could possibly happen to you? Our need for control stems from fear which prevents us from letting go (Marianne Williamson).

I have had several dreams over the years when I was free falling in each one. One time I was in a lift that had broken, another time I was on a sledge out of control. The same thing always happened: my fall was always cushioned and I felt at peace and fully protected.

During my reiki 2 training I felt I was falling back into the abyss; my logical part told me I was out of control and so I clawed my way back out. I was unable to let go.

Complete surrendering is about losing control. Branden Bays talks about her experience of falling back through the layers, completely surrendering into (it) or source or whatever fits with your belief system. Letting go to be caught in the loving embrace of God. This, for me is still a work in progress.

Losing control is very hard for a lot of us, it is a matter of faith and trust. I have it on good authority that all of us will be caught. I have even experienced it in my dreams. We are totally supported at all times by the higher realms.

Writing down your feelings seems to unblock resistance and fear of letting go, holding on takes up energy and is tiring and prevents full access to source and to intuition (Marianne Williamson). The process involves getting out of our way and be led by the wisdom of the body. (Guidance form the Path of Soul destiny cards by Cheryl Lee Harnish, number 32, Nurturing Universe)

Being divinely nurtured and supported calls for us to allow full flow of energy within us to nurture and support us. The healing energy is available at all times. This nurturing feminine energy will soothe you and guide you onto your path.

Loneliness and Feeling Down

An emotion is only an emotion. It is not the actual event that caused the unpleasant feeling.

We often distract ourselves and fill the gaps from the unpleasantness of feeling lonely and down, but the problem with this is that the feelings follow us around until we acknowledge them and deal with them. One of the ways to address this is to not fill the gap, be in it, feel it, do not distract yourself from it, do not reach for the bottle or the drugs either prescribed or 'recreational' as a quick fix. This just often dulls the senses and stops the process or alters the perception without strengthening the mind. This is a time for courage not escape because there is no escape until you face it and deal with it.

It is time to bring out the tools and use them. It's a time to practise the yoga, Reiki, meditation, nature, creativity, etc. Yet how often do we abandon our tools just when we need them the most?

Try to use the tools without being attached to the outcome, carry on carrying on. Knowing that one day you will see light at the end of the tunnel and in fact as the saying goes the darkest hour comes before the dawn, also the footprints in the sand poem is about one set of footprints as being the time we are carried.

Remember Franscesca's mantra "this too will pass" meaning the good and the bad so enjoy the good while it lasts and know that the bad won't last for ever. Use it as an opportunity to grow and to develop. It's a time for acceptance and patience. If we sit still, then our deepest desires are allowed to manifest. If our desires are unfulfilled then they become a yearning until they are suppressed, eventually these become dispersed as we try and fill the gap of our suppressed desires, but the gap can't be filled and it doesn't go away, it just becomes locked in the body in the unconscious. So go back to the beginning, feel, unlock the desire and allow it into your life.

When I eventually sat still after years of distraction and frenetic activity, the tools came forth to help me unleash my stored up desires, my deepest wish unfolded before me. My journey back to horses as healers and teachers began, bringing with it fulfilment.

Affirmations are very helpful in this process, even if you don't feel anything just carry on with your positive affirmation about yourself. There is a lovely poem that uses the analogy of a sour grape becoming a sweet mature grape resulting in a fine wine through our suffering. Our deepest love and compassion is the end result of our suffering.

Self-denial

I was in constant denial, continually distracting myself with activities and exercise, ignoring the messages my body was trying to give me. As time went on, more issues were stored in the body as I had not dealt with them. The glass of issues fills up slowly until one day it overflows and the container can no longer cope. This is when we have the breakdown or as some would prefer to call it – a breakthrough. We can no longer cope, our usual strategies fail and we have to deal with our issues. As a very wise holistic therapist said to me, we cannot do the inner work and the outer work at the same time. Meaning sometimes we need time off work in order to deal with our unresolved issues from the past.

There comes a time when we have to stop and listen to the messages from the body and we often wait until these are screaming at us. Emotional issues if not dealt with can progress into physical illness. "Your Body Speaks Your mind" by Debbie Shapiro is an excellent resource book to help you to decipher the messages your body is giving you about your internal emotional hidden world. After all the body is where the memory calls home. All your aches and pains and illnesses are the body trying to tell you something, are you listening?

This is a time to access your regular tool box along with your occasional tools, and even some you have not yet tried but present themselves for special occasions, such as breakthrough times. Yoga provides a way of learning to listen to the body's messages and becoming familiar and at home in your body. It never ceases to amaze me how we inhabit a body all our lives and yet have little idea what it's telling us.

I stored a lot of my unresolved past issues in my back, I have had numerous back injuries and accidents over the years and always had backache. I could not sit on a chair without back support for even short periods because of the back ache. Some people can store issues in their backs unconsciously so that no one can see them. We present our front view to the world and it appears all is well.

Bringing awareness to the breath and simple meditation allows us insight into our inner world as we close down our internal mental chatter and external noise overload from the busy outside world along with its distractions, deadlines and negative news. Meditation lets us know how we really feel.

In order to meditate you need to have an unsupported straight back but I could not go deep or sit for long periods because of the backache, so I found myself in a no-win situation. A resolution came with a chair recommended by an osteopath in order to provide support for my lower back, I could then sit comfortably for long periods and over time established a deeper meditation practice and one by one my back issues that were emotional as well as physical came to the surface to be released and resolved bit by bit.

As well as the chair and meditation other tools that facilitated this healing included, Chiropractors then McTimmoney chiropractors, Hatha Yoga especially Yin yoga which works on an emotional level , reflexology, counselling,

EFT and Vibro-Harmonization Technique (VHT).

I can now sit for long periods of time, unsupported without backache. I no longer need any treatment and maintain a healthy back with yoga, meditation, and VHT, first developed by Jock Ruddock.

Shame

It was during my breakthrough when I felt great shame for needing to take time off work. Everyone was very kind to me as I was ill and the only one that wasn't kind to me was me! Anyone else I would have offered my support, but not for me. Why is this? Why are we so hard on ourselves? I felt somehow weak and expected more from myself even though a friend pointed out how we can all be vulnerable at some period in our lives and we all need support sometime.

The hardest part for me was taking the first step and it took the counsellor to spell it out to me that I was ill and needed to be off sick. Once I was off I then realised just how ill I had become and couldn't even read a book I was so tired. The further you fall before seeking help, the farther it is to drag yourself up and the longer it takes to recover from the battle field of life.

I was ashamed of being unable to cope; me, being a stress management trainer after all. I was weak, I should have been stronger. Yet, being off with stress doesn't really mean anything, it is just a collection of symptoms. In the western culture some of us self-destruct, using negative support such as drugs or alcohol to survive. Or, we distract ourselves through our work which is slowly working us to death. Life is meant to be joyful.

I think shame is embedded within cultures and ancestral patterns ie "The Victorian work ethic". We also allow other people's opinions of us to affect us, yet really other people's opinion of us is none of our business; we needn't concern ourselves with **their** opinion of us. We really need to work on **our** opinion of ourselves.

Some suggestions for dealing with shame includes: EFT- tap on feelings of shame. Transcend the ego and rise above it, do not be afraid to speak your truth, try having a different opinion than previous generations - make up your own mind, have the best intentions, work for the highest good, come from a place of love, love yourself, and know that other people are not always that wise (however old they may be), just even more entrenched with their views. If people don't deal with their issues, they just become more fixed over time and, like cement, they become stuck.

Ancestral patterns

I believe that some ancestral patterns do not serve us or society very well, some are dysfunctional. That dysfunction can magnify and become more entrenched through the generations. If we can recognise these patterns, then we can begin to do something about it, begin to undo them and behave differently, more healthily. If we manage to achieve this, not only do we heal ourselves, stop the pattern continuing for the generations to come, but also heal the past generations.

Once we recognise the pattern, we can act differently, give a different example to our children and society of how to act towards each other, be kinder, always coming from love and respect for each other.

As Ghandi said:

"Be the change you would like to see in the world."

In other words, we can **only** change ourselves. But, we can be an example to other people, either for good or for bad.

Feeling overwhelmed with life!

Can't see the wood for the trees? Too busy, feeling totally overwhelmed? Then here are some useful tools to help you look at your life and make it more manageable and more enjoyable.

Life mapping helps you to have an overview of your life and break down areas that suit you and aspects that don't. It helps you to start seeing the individual branches. Using a separate bubble for each area of your life, put a smiley face by what you like more of and a frown face by what you would like less of. From your frowns, put numbers by them for you to prioritise what you would like to change first. Then, use an action planning tool to help organise your time.

A selection of techniques I have found useful are shown overleaf. Life-mapping can be useful for developing projects or planning your future.

Life Map

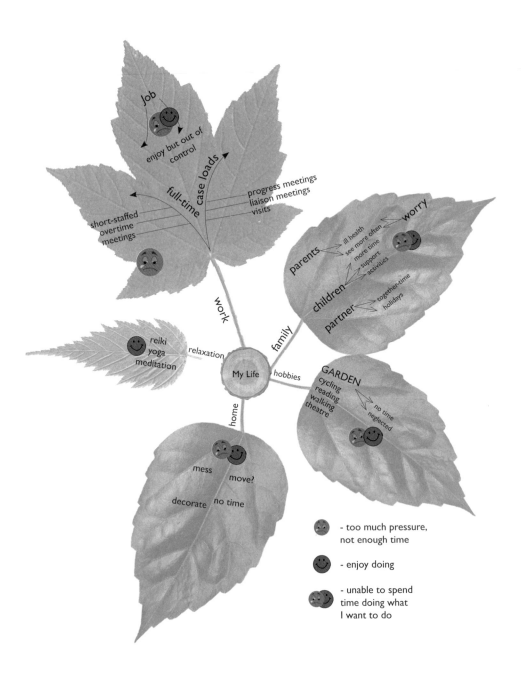

Job
enjoy but out of control
case loads
full-time
progress meetings
liaison meetings
visits
short-staffed
overtime
meetings

work

parents
ill health
see more often
more time
support
activities
worry
children
partner
together-time
holidays

family

reiki
yoga
meditation
relaxation

My Life

hobbies

GARDEN
cycling
reading
walking
theatre
no time
neglected

home

mess
move?
decorate
no time

- too much pressure, not enough time

- enjoy doing

- unable to spend time doing what I want to do

46

Your Life Map

Map out the key areas of your life. Notice the areas of conflict. These are the areas that need working on. Once you have done this, prioritise. Use the action plan overleaf to help you.

work

family

relaxation

hobbies

home

Action Plan Table

To balance my life/the action I took

Issue	What	When	Where	How	Who
1. Finances	Budgeting: can I manage on less?	By next month.	Bank account	Spend less, budget, pay less.	Me

EXAMPLE 1

Questions to ask yourself: 1. What can I do alone?
2. What can I do with others?
3. What can others do for me?

Continuum

On a scale of 1-10, how much are you in control of your life now?

1   5   10

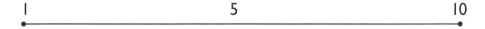

What changes do you need to make in order to get to 10?

How will you know when you have got there?

Visioning

Visioning is a helpful tool.

What is your vision for your life?

What would you like to happen?

Ask for help/you are never alone/look for your signs to guide you.

Meditate before you make decisions to gain clarity - this is the key to everything.
Do not make big decisions in an emotional state.

Steps to take

**vision
balance
wellbeing**

Feel more
relaxed.

More free
time.

Good social
life.

Feeling fitter.

Budgeting the
finances.

Taking more
control of life.

Cook own
meals.

Join a walking
group.

Plenty of sleep.

Reduce work-
ing hours.
Part-time
or change job.

Food diary.
Vegetarian?

Reduce work-
load.

Healthy eating.

Exercise.

Recognise the
need to
become more
balanced.

1 2 3 4 5

Fill in your own steps:

**vision
balance
wellbeing**

1 2 3 4 5

50

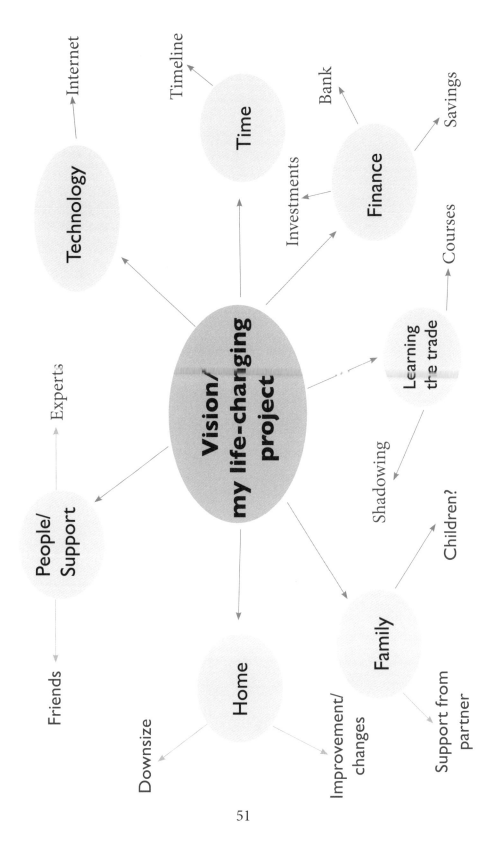

51

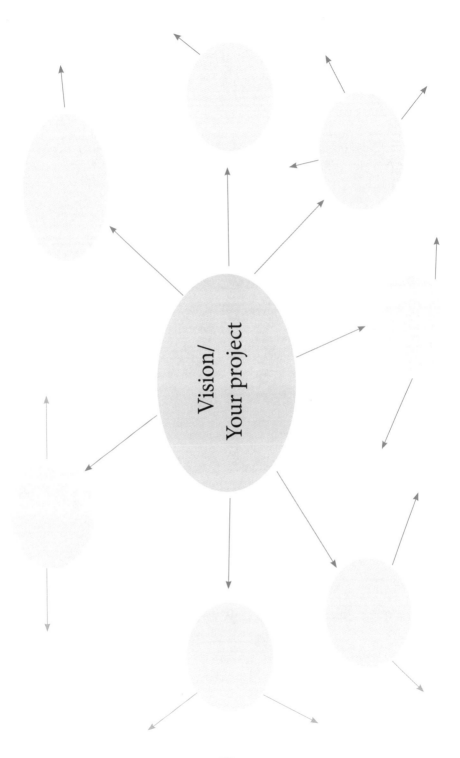

Timeline

Date	Actions

Jan Meeting with management.   Business plan
        Look at reducing hours part-time.
        Look at other jobs?

Feb appointment with bank/financial   Support from others?
        advisor

Mar   Make the changes/make it happen

Apr Begin to take control of your own time.   shadowing
        Take time to relax.

May Meet new people   Exercise/Diet

Jun   Join walking groups, gym, yoga group.
                    class.

Jul   Gardening/art class

Aug

Sep   Training course/new job

Oct
        Downsize/lodger

Nov   Look back: is the plan working?

Dec   Maybe look at other models?

        Feeling in control, no pressure,
        Relaxed

        HAPPY

Part 2

Relationships

and

Interactions

Friendships

*F*riendships can be tricky until we remove our veils and see clearly. Until then, it is difficult to judge what is true friendship and healthy and what isn't and unhealthy.

As we begin to unfold and grow, some friendships will grow alongside in sync with each other, some will not. We may start off together but grow farther apart over time. This is the time to let go and move on which may feel quite painful but needs to be done for each other to grow personally and spiritually. Who knows, in time, the old friends may become new again.

These are some questions that may help you to assess your friendships:

*   Is it just a habit?
*   Is it healthy, do you enjoy each others company?
*   What are the motives of your friends and your own motives?
*   Are you both developing and growing in your friendship?
*   Does your friend have your best interests at heart and vice-versa?
*   Do you have things in common?
*   Are you hanging on for historic reasons?

- Does it need to alter, can it be altered?
- Is it time to let go?

Our friends may come into our lives at certain times for a reason, to teach us the lessons we need to learn, but the reason may have served its purpose. Sometimes the friendship continues but is different, and at other times we have to let go in order for the new to come into our lives. I have had to let go of several friends, some by letter, cards, phone calls, detachment, discussion, emails. Some have let go of me.

Some are easier to let go of than others, some may have held power over us for a long time without us knowing. There may be co-dependency with others that is holding us both back, or we may be feeding each others insecurities and difficulties.

Souls journey together, weaving in and out of life's rich tapestry but our journey is our journey and their journey is their journey. Sometimes we have to go it alone for a while.

The journey can be lonely until we learn to be at one with our aloneness and connect to source. I look back in gratitude and give huge thanks to my friends, both past and present, for their love and support and also for some painful and difficult lessons they have taught me along the way. Without them, I would not be where I am now.

Remember, we can choose our friends but we cannot choose our family.

Sometimes we have to journey alone but remember, we are never truly alone we are always supported and guided from the higher realms; we just need to trust and look for the signs.

Letting go of friends that are no longer good for us

When it is time to journey apart for our mutual growth, there are many ways to approach it. Here are some:

- Just detach and say nothing unless you are asked.
- Write a letter or email.
- Have the conversation on the phone.
- Arrange to meet for lunch.

Different friends will warrant different approaches. In order to decide the right one, listen to your body, see it from an eagle-eyed perspective, meditate to gain clarity, come from love, use EFT to tap on any emotions. There may be some grief and feelings of loss. This is quite normal and EFT is of great benefit.

If choosing to meet up, it is useful to practice by visualising the interaction. Watch your posture. Are you confident with shoulders back and standing tall? If you look the part you will begin to feel it. Practise what you will say and how you will say it; be clear what message you are going to give. Think about what their reply may be and how you will respond and be clear what outcome you would like to achieve.

When the time arrives, use a sandwich way of explaining yourself so that you start with a positive. Any negative is in the middle, then you end on a positive note. This could include sharing your good memories and the mutual support, explaining how the friendship is no longer of mutual benefit and you are growing apart. Then, finish with how you will always have fond memories of your time together but now it is better for both of you to go your own separate ways and you wish them all the best for the future. If the person expresses anger or sadness, be empathic and kind but do not weaken. This is a test, stay true to yourself. Be kind, but firm and implacable in your decision.

I experienced a really interesting visualisation in my meditation on this theme. The trunk of my body was a garden and certain people represented different aspects in my garden. These included thorns in my side and prickles, dead wood that was stuck and needed digging out from the roots, vines wrapped around my body confining me and squeezing the life out of me, poo and little weeds and a patch of barren sand in which I fertilised the soil and planted a tangerine rose.

This theme continued and after my friendships had been altered or pruned mutually I had a dream where my body was now black rich fertile soil ready for planting. I had to detach and empty in order to refill with lots of colourful friendships. My guidance recently has been to start adding lots of different colours to my garden in order for it to flourish. Only last week I received a bouquet of tangerine roses from a friend who did not know about my garden. Sometimes old friends may in the future become new friends again, once mutual growth has taken place.

We need to take time to prune and weed, feed the soil

then plant our seeds and observe and nurture the growth, creating favourable conditions in order to flourish in life.

A sankalpa (used in yoga) is a way of setting our intention for what we would like in our life. Decide what you would like, then, when relaxed, say it to yourself three times with feeling and intensity and know that this will happen. Keep the same sankalpa until it manifests.

Ask, wait and allow, letting go of any resistance. **The universe has abundance and is waiting to give it to you!** (E, Hicks. J, Hicks, 2010) (R., Byrne. 2006)

The universe also knows best so, if you do not receive what you are asking for, it may be because there is something better for you just round the corner.

Friends
The passive-agressors and the rescuers

Passive-agressive 'friends' try to persuade you to do things or get you involved in their problems, or offload their problems when it isn't your problem.

Alberto Villoldo in "Conscious Dreaming" suggests asking yourself if you are any of the following: a bully, victim or rescuer, and if so, change it.

This is quite a challenge to deal with, as they often ask you to become involved with a smile or exclaim "Only you can do!" or "I know I can rely on you!" or "You are better at it than I am!". Does this sound familiar? These are their weapons. They are well-practised at manipulating situations in order to get what they want and appealing to your caring nature, pulling at your heart strings. This is a form of aggression, just delivered in a passive way.

Some tips for dealing with this:

• Remove yourself from the drama, as if viewing yourself in the audience, whilst you act your part on stage in a play and observe the interaction.
• Be prepared, ground your feet, observe your body's

reaction, bring awareness to the breath. Count to 10 before replying.

- Try saying no whilst maintaining a positive relationship. Sometimes the "no" needs to be emphatic (not aggressive).
- "Broken record" technique – repeating the same phrase until they get it.
- Give it back to them and ask what they think they could do to solve their problem and to help themselves.
- The answers are within us, we just have to peel away the layers like an onion, to get down to the real issue.
- Give yourself time to think before agreeing to anything.
- Try a different response if the one you give does not work.
- Rise above it and see it from a different perspective.
- If you are working harder than they are to solve their problem, then think again.

Manipulation

People who expect more of you than you
either can or are willing to give.

This, again, can be difficult and before you know it, you could be giving more than you have to offer:

- Be clear what you are prepared to offer.
- Have clear boundaries.
- How much time you can give and when?
- Ask them what they intend to do to help themselves.
- Who else could help them?
- What plan do they have to get well or improve their situation?
- Would they like some suggestions of what/who may help? Books, therapists or classes?

Remember that their journey is their journey, we can support without getting embroiled in their journey. Your journey is your journey and unique to you. You have a choice and you can choose how to react. If it does not work, then try something different. Feelings of guilt can be tapped on, using EFT.

Weapons that may be used to manipulate you:

- People may use emotional blackmail, trying to make you feel guilty or that it is your responsibility. They may act pathetic/helpless/weeping, so you will give in. Some people are "energy vampires" and can suck the life out of you. A technique to support and protect yourself with this, is to imagine there is a white light around you.
- Another weapon used by others is to deliver poison whilst smiling sweetly, so what they are saying does not match what they are meaning or feeling. Watch out for this, as it can be very well hidden. The expression of a "wolf in sheep's clothing" comes to mind.
- If people dig their own hole, do not be tempted to jump into it with them, this won't be helpful to anyone. They won't learn their lesson and you will end up as stuck as they are. You can, however, offer support and give suggestions from above their hole.

People you find challenging
are often your greatest teachers

People who push our buttons

We all know the ones, those who "make" us feel angry, humiliated and a range of other unpleasant emotions.

The good news is that no one can **make** us feel anything. We have a choice, we can choose how we feel and we can also choose how we react to situations. So, the next time someone pushes your buttons, choose how you are going to react.

Feel into your body and try a different way of reacting from your usual way and observe how that feels in your body. Also, observe how the other person reacts to you now you have chosen something different. This way, you have gained some control over the situation.

Eckhart Tolle in "The Power of Now" writes a lot about this and suggests staying in the present moment, giving yourself time to think of your reaction, giving gentle eye contact, not feeding the other person by reacting. I have followed his suggestions and it works.

Being criticised pushes my buttons. In the past, I would react defensively but underneath feel unworthy and humiliated, so now instead of defending my corner, I allow the criticism, I stay present, I observe how I feel in my body, giving kind eye contact. By not reacting in the usual way, this tends to disarm the person and the situation does not escalate. At first, the criticism from the other person may increase, but staying present and choosing how to react alters everything. In one situation I was asked if I was mellowing in my old age. I replied: "No, I am just choosing another way of reacting". During this particular interaction I continued to feel into the body.

If feeling into the body is difficult, as it can be for some people, a yoga class helps you to inhabit the body and listen to the messages constantly being given. Tuning into the body helps us to gauge if our reaction is healthy for us or if it brings uncomfortable feelings with it. If it does, then try another approach and keep trying something different until it feels better.

Another pattern of mine was to match verbal aggression towards me with the same reaction, which always quickly escalated the situation and caused me stress. Hence the expression "causing my blood to boil", as the adrenaline surged around the body.

When I chose to react differently to this, I was able to stand back and observe the feelings in my body and observe the reaction of the other person along with the de-escalation of the situation. Some of the ways I tried included:

- Time out counting from anything from 1 to 100.
- Choosing how to react.
- Choosing when to react, sometimes saying "I will consider my reply and get back to you."
- Not replying in an emotional state.
- Bringing awareness to my breath, creating my

"breathing space".

- Choosing how to reply. It may be spoken or written in a creative way.

The steps I have just listed help us to have control over the situation which, in turn, enables us to feel more confident and empowered. Being able to communicate effectively evens out any power imbalance, instead of leaving us powerless or having power over another. We are empowered and in a position to negotiate and express our feelings, thoughts and wishes in an adult-to-adult way, rather than child-to-adult.

In other words, I may choose to react assertively but the key word here is **choose**- I have control, I can choose not to react angrily.

Again, the body is a great barometer to find out how we are feeling. Remember, we have lots of tools to help us to work through the uncomfortable feelings and emotions. These Include EFT, which works like magic within minutes. Our bodies give us a lot of useful information. Hatha yoga is very helpful, enabling us to become more present within our bodies, therefore being able to read the signs and messages it sends us.

Anger/Unacceptable Behaviour/ Unpredictable behaviour

Ekhart Tolle in "The Power of Now"(2001) discusses some very useful techniques to support us in dealing with difficult situations:

- Do not react angrily, it only feeds it.
- Feel into your body.
- Bring awareness to the breath.
- Give gentle eye contact throughout – not defiant or hostile.
- Not reacting disarms the situation.
- Choose how and when to get your point across.
- Be calm and assertive.
- Do not be afraid.
- Send love from the heart.
- Be totally present.

People in Authority

If someone in authority does not like you or you do not like them, ask yourself why that might be. Could there be some mirroring going on? Is it because people in authority have the power? Does it remind you of a previous experience, does the same experience keep following you around and does it make you automatically become defensive? Is it a pattern and does the pattern keep repeating itself?

Would you like a different pattern with a different outcome? Are you getting bored with this one? Ask yourself what the lesson might be.

Then, try something different. Start by observing how you feel, be more open and less defensive, alter your attitude, change your body language, tone of voice, expectations, believe that you will get on. You will be amazed at how quickly the situation changes for the better, even without saying anything.

What would you like to happen? Would you like to be involved in the decision making, be able to discuss issues on a level playing field? Perhaps feel that you have some control and self-empowerment?

Workaholic managers

I had one of these once; they were on a slippery slope to becoming ill and I made a decision I wasn't going to join them. Some techniques I found useful were:

- Imagine a white light round me and one round the office before I entered.
- I made a decision a long time ago that the NHS wasn't going to kill me because if I let it, it would.
- I had clear boundaries and was very clear what I was and was not prepared to do.
- I did the work within the time available.
- Established the balance between work and home.
- Worked mindfully.
- Created a nice work space.

A friend of mine had a manipulative, workaholic manager and this was a pattern in her life. She began to sort it out by recognising that she had a lesson to learn. She practised what she would say, what she wanted to achieve and tried saying "no" in different ways whilst maintaining a positive relationship. She chose how to react and gave herself time to react. She observed him attempting to manipulate her by rising above the drama.

Sometimes we need to make judgements about people in order to keep ourselves safe and well. It is useful to ask yourself what the motivations of the other person are, what your motivations are and always come from a place of love. Scott Peck covers this in his book entitled "People of the lie".

I had a pattern in my life of being at the mercy of unstable men, even to a point of being stalked and I did the usual thing of burying my head in the sand. In order to alter the pattern, I decided to change what I normally did. I was assertive and dealt with the situation. Throughout the unpleasant episode my mantra was:

"And the truth will set you free"
...and it did!

It was out of this situation that I devised my own body warning system to alert me to any signs of danger in the future. My body is very reliable and has a built-in warning system. Now all I have to do is to listen to it and take appropriate action. Simple.

I have included this here as an example, complete with numbers and colour codes. You may find it useful to develop your own system depending on your signs that are particular to you. Your body labelled with feelings of stress is a start.

As already discussed with regards to the earlier body drawing (page 26), a useful way of breaking down how you feel is to write onto the diagram the feelings you feel and thoughts you have when under pressure. It helps you to become more

All well   **Warning signs**   **Danger**

1	2	3	4	5	6	7	8	9	10

1–3 (All well):
- OK
- No fear
- Love
- Joy
- Relaxed
- Energised
- Effective
- Enjoy life

4–6 (Warning signs):
- Biting nails/skin
- Stomach butterflies
- Bury my head
- Tense solar plexus
- Busy head
- Tense bladder
- Uncomfortable emotions
- Tredness/can't eat
- Headache
- Uneasiness/disquiet
- Diarrhoea
- Skin problems

7–8 (Warning signs):
- Fear in bladder
- Very tired
- Repulsed
- Panic
- Stress-induced asthma
- Weight loss
- Sweating
- Prone to illness
- Meditation difficult
- Back ache
- Tearful
- Embarrassment

9–10 (Danger):
- Unable to function
- Exhausted
- Crying
- Solar plexus sore
- Can't read
- Can't focus
- Distracted
- Palpitations
- Fast pulse
- Impossible
- Dread
- Fear

77

Now, fill in your own early warning
systems, based on your completed
body diagram. (p. 26)

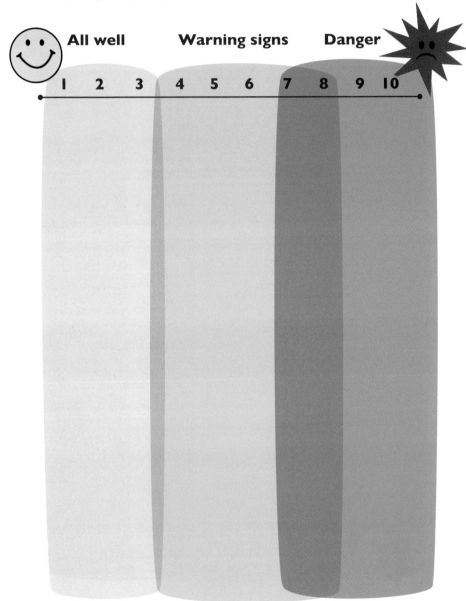

aware of your own warning signs and tune into your body's messages.

Bullying

Bullying has been a recurring theme in my life. It is learnt behaviour, either by being a bully or being bullied. In my experience, people will often admit to the latter but not the former. In reality, they sometimes go hand-in-hand.

Bullying in the workplace

Bullying in organisations is widespread. It can be found at all levels and in any department. In my own experience, I noticed that the same old pattern kept repeating itself until I eventually recognised it for what it was and dealt with it differently. It appeared in different jobs, locations, in different ways, but it was still bullying.

Usual pattern

My usual way of dealing with bullying was to bury my head or have an angry outburst or, if either of those didn't work, I would leave and get another job but, guess what, it would happen again. And on I would go, on the same old merry-go-round until I got the gist of it!

Eventually the penny dropped. In order to be free of the pattern, I needed to react differently. I decided to try a different approach. Life is not an exact science so if something doesn't work, try something different and see how that works out.

Breaking the pattern

In "Conscious Dreaming" (2009), Alberto Villoldo suggests that you ask yourself if, at any time, you are either a victim, rescuer or bully, in order to alter the pattern.

In this instance, the bullying was happening in public meetings. My body was telling me how uncomfortable I felt but it wasn't until a lay person mentioned that there was bullying going on that I realised what the problem was. I mentioned it to my manager who suggested I had a word with the person. My alert warning system, had I had it in place at that time, would have been 6-7, depending on the severity.

Techniques

Before I spoke to the person, I visualised what I would say, how I would look, what my posture might look like, what the other person would say to me, what I would reply, what outcome I wanted. I also practised bringing awareness to my breathing, which is helpful for releasing tension and having control in a situation.

I had a quiet word with the person who had no awareness of her actions. In fact, she had previously been given positive feedback on how she conducted meetings. In bullying cultures this behaviour is often reinforced: aggression and assertiveness get mixed up. We discussed how I presented myself, which she felt was confrontational, probably because I had the best intentions but felt disempowered. We discussed what we could both learn from the experience and how we could both work together in the future, in a more productive manner. I came out of the meeting feeling confident, empowered and very pleased with the outcome. It felt like a win-win situation. The future meetings were conducted differently; they became a healthier and more conducive environment. Most importantly, I learnt the lesson and it stopped following me around. It also allowed the other person to grow both personally and professionally. Feedback from others attending the meetings indicated that they felt listened to, were more relaxed and that actions were met more effectively.

Questions to prompt you:

- Are there any recurring themes in your life you wish to alter?
- Is your body giving you any warning signals? What are these? What is your score?
- What can you try differently?
- How can you prepare yourself? What techniques can you use?
- What support have you got?
- When will you try your new pattern?
- What are you hoping to achieve?
- How will you know when you have got there?

Key points

I realise that the areas covered in these pages are not an exhaustive list of all the different scenarios we are faced with on a daily basis. That would be impossible to achieve, as we are all different people facing a range of challenges. However, the selection of examples I have chosen highlights some of the methods to use in order to navigate the maze of life.

They are useful techniques that are transferrable across a wide range of interactions and situations depending on your lessons. The point of our journey is to wake up and become conscious. Once we are conscious and understand ourselves, we are better equipped to deal with our uncomfortable emotions, our ancestral patterns and personalities. We have our tool kit to help us and remind us that if something doesn't work, we must try something different. Treat life as an intensive training course, experimenting with new approaches and new ways of being.

When it comes to relationships, a lot of the difficulties arise from power and powerlessness, manipulation, fear of the consequences and criticism

We must be able to negotiate and change the balance of power onto an even playing field. Never give our power to another or have blind faith in people and situations.

Recognise manipulation and do not accept it by reacting differently. If you use the appropriate techniques, as discussed, then you will have some control over the situation, which in turn, will be less stressful and as a result, give the opportunity to turn fear into love. Always come from a place of love.

Have enough self-worth, confidence and clear boundaries not to agree with the criticism. We can, however reflect on the critics' point of view. By doing this, we will continue to grow and develop, moving from the darkness into the light, bringing with it freedom and liberation from the bonds of delusion.

When we first free ourselves from the drama of life, we can feel a little lost, until we start to feel our connection to source. At this time, just keep on having faith, trust and know that the way will open.

Below is a re-cap on some of the key points:

- Ask for help and guidance from the higher realms and look for the signs, listen to messages in dreams, books, teachers and meditation.
- Use your tool kit, keep adding to it.
- Be totally present.
- Feel into the body and listen to any messages.
- Pay attention to your early alarm signals and act on them.
- View difficult people as your teachers. Ask yourself what the lesson is.
- Choose how to react.
- If a reaction doesn't work, try something different.
- Be in the drama, then step off the stage and observe it from the audience.

- Rise above the situation.
- Don't make decisions and/or reply in an emotional state.
- Come from a place of love.
- Ask yourself what the motivation of the other person is.
- View life as an intensive training course.
- If the same lesson keeps coming, ask yourself why. Do you need to react differently?
- Be careful what you wish for, thoughts are powerful.
- Seek awareness within. Develop your intuition.
- Being is as essential as doing.
- Use discrimination when making decisions.

Nature

The beauty the colours the stillness in nature,
connecting me to my soul,
connecting me to the divine.

The wildness and beauty of the moors,
the changing of the seasons and the colours,
the clarity of the light.

Moors in spring, golden straw,
moors in summer rich green,

Autumn colours golden bronze
into winter pale straw.

The sense of space wild and free.
The rhythm of life with the rhythm of the seasons.

Peace within, peace without.
Nature as a form of meditation.
My connection to the land expressed as a poem...

by J E Taylor

Part 3

Wellbeing

My Wellbeing/Health Pie Chart

When my wheel is balanced, this then has an automatic knock-on effect or bearing with the rest of my life/work/family etc.

Your Wellbeing/Health Pie Chart

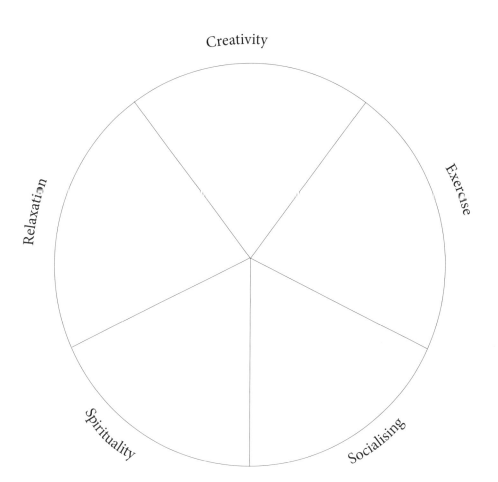

Below are definitions of *selfish* and *selfless*. We are aiming for somewhere in-between the two - **balance**.

selfish | adjective: Concerned mainly with one's own needs or wishes at the expense of consideration for other people. (Oxford Dictionary)
selfless | adjective: Concerned more with the needs and wishes of other people than with one's own. (Oxford Dictionary)

Some people have difficulty in completing the health pie, especially women, as they often feel that thinking of themselves is selfish and they should be there for everyone else, but not for themselves.

But, by doing this, it gives the example to others that your needs are not important and that other people's needs should be fulfilled at the expense of your own.

If you do not meet your needs, then how can you offer anything to anyone else? You are just as important and have as much right as other members of your family to feel well and healthy and have some time to yourself.

You are an example to your family of how to **be** in the world. This cannot be fulfilled when ill, feeling resentful or offering yourself up as a martyr or rescuer. Remember, we need to love ourselves before we can give that love to all.

So, in order to be well and healthy, all aspects of the health pie need to be addressed. Which of yours are currently being met and which are in need of your attention? What can you do to achieve it?

Feeling daunted? Then, look at a gap and plan to take a small step towards making a change that will bring you joy. You may need to negotiate and compromise within the family. It is all about balance. Remember Ghandi's saying:

"Be the change you want to see in the world."

Ask yourself: "Are you the change you want to see in the world?"

Meditation – the key

*B*reath awareness/meditation is the key to everything! It is no accident that people say "I need some breathing space", meaning - time out to think and to heal. The breath creates the space, which allows the body and mind to relax and let go, gaining some clarity of thought. Once we find the stillness within, our intuition can develop, rather than being led by the mind. Meditation helps us to have a shift in the mind and to strengthen the mind.

It is within the pauses at the end of the in-breath and the end of the out-breath, that time stands still and expansion occurs within the silence and the non-doing.

People can often be very resistant to meditation, especially in the West, stating that they cannot do it, do not know how to do it, have not got the time to do it, don't see the benefit or do not know where to start.

My answer to all of that is to start somewhere. You don't need to be perfect or have all the answers. Just be happy where you are right now. Start from here, start now, with a simple breath-awareness exercise, even if it is just 5 minutes a day, set the alarm clock 5 mins earlier, swing your legs off the end of the bed, place your feet flat on the floor or sit on a straight-backed chair, chin slightly pointing down, eyes gently shut, palms on your lap, facing upwards. Be warm and comfortable. Now choose a technique which concentrates the mind and/or synchronises the breath. Here is an example:

•   Breathe in through the nose, tense the whole body, hold for a few seconds, then breathe out and relax. Repeat another couple of times.

•   Now breathe in through your nose and, as you do ,mentally chant to yourself: "I am breathing in" -- pause -- then, breathe out through the nose while chanting: "I am breathing out"-- pause --.

•   Continue with that for the next few minutes. If the mind wanders, as it often does, don't beat yourself up. Instead, just acknowledge that it has wandered and bring it back to the breath-awareness exercise.

•   At the end of a few minutes, just sit in the silence. Enjoy the peace.

There is no competition, so try not to be attached to any outcome; just sit and practise the technique. Plan your next session: same time every day works well for some people as this becomes part of the routine, alongside brushing your hair, cleaning your teeth, and breath-awareness.

When I first started meditating, I was unable to sit for any period of time and needed support from the back of the chair. I found it difficult to concentrate because of backache as I have previously discussed. I found a really comfortable straight-backed chair recommended by an osteopath, which gave my lower back a lot more support.

Over time, this enabled me to sit for longer periods of time and go deeper in my meditation, which spontaneously allowed me to begin releasing old issues subconsciously stored in my back, out of sight. I can now sit for longer periods, without needing the support of the back of the chair, which is a more favourable position to be able to sit in. For me it was a bit like the "chicken and the egg" scenario. Which comes first? I could not sit long enough to go deep in meditation but until I could, it was difficult for me to release the stuck issues within my body which, incidentally, I had not known were there to start with.

Other tools that helped me to release issues within the body were McTimmoney chiropractor, Hatha yoga, EFT and reflexology. The list of some of the benefits I have experienced over the years from meditation include:

- Clarity of thought, decision making.
- Relaxation, managing stress.
- Releasing old issues.
- Becoming a witness to my thoughts realising I am not my thoughts.
- Sitting in deep peace and silence.
- Releasing old patterns of thought.
- Understanding myself and my purpose in life.
- Developing intuition.
- Recognising how I feel right now.
- Deep healing.

My advice to anyone would be to start somewhere and start today. In my experience, it is the secret to surviving life!

Try not to be attached to any outcome, do not expect anything. If you are meditating regularly and think it is not doing anything, just keep on trying, it will be having an effect you are just not conscious of it yet. The effects are very subtle.

Staying Well

There seem to be people on opposite ends of the spectrum: at one end, there are those that hand their body over to the medical model for invasive investigative procedures and/or take a plethora of prescription drugs. I am not suggesting medication is all bad. Sometimes it is necessary, but like everything we have been given to use, it is about the integrity with which it is used.

Then, at the other end of the spectrum, are those who ignore all attempts of the body to alert them to potential problems and wait until they are almost dead, before seeking assistance or altering any aspect of their lifestyle/behaviour.

For some strange reason, some people have stopped taking responsibility for their own health and have handed their bodies over to "those who know best". Except, in a lot of cases we know best, as we inhabit our bodies 100% of the time. All we have to do is to tune into the signals and modify any behaviours that are not healthy for us and seek appropriate support at the appropriate time, in order to nudge the body to heal itself.

Case study

A colleague recently told me how her stomach was swollen and she was about to undergo investigations to find the problem. When asked if she had perhaps looked at her diet and kept a food diary and eliminated foods that may not agree with her to see if anything was causing the bloating, it turned out she had not; however, she had an idea that it may be her consumption of red wine that may be causing the problem, but hadn't yet decreased her intake of red wine. She would rather undergo investigations than take responsibility for her own health. Perhaps some aspect of the medical model has encouraged us to become dependent, passive recipients of care, rather than active doers.

Some questions to ask yourself:

- How much responsibility do you take regarding your own health and wellbeing?
- Do you participate in your own care of yourself?
- Are you a partner in the care of yourself with any health professionals such as a GP or a nurse?
- Are there any negative lifestyle choices that you would like to change?
- Could you make a list of what you would like to change, prioritise your list and start with the first one, make a plan?
- Are there any positive lifestyle choices you could add?
- Are you listening to your body?
- Do you want to add any more tools that may help i.e relaxation, yoga, Reiki, complimentary therapies?

Some suggestions for health and wellbeing:

- Start simple. We are what we eat, so keep a food diary. "Optimum Nutrition Made Easy" by Patrick Holford is a really useful book with regards to nutrition.
- Choose how to react to stressful situations.
- Be guided by your intuition as it develops.
- Seek advice and support as needed, choose the model of support that suits you and the occasion.
- Access the cause of the problem - not just the symptoms.

Spiritual Path

Everyone has one!

There are many paths that lead to the same place. It is important that people find their own path that is right for them and only the individual will know it. I remained very open, listened to lots of people and read widely until my path presented itself clearly to me. Look for, and find your own spiritual path.

Once you have your path, the way becomes very narrow; just follow the teachings given to you. You now have your sail, compass and navigator. Sometimes the waters are calm and other times we have to navigate choppy waters; sometimes even choppier than before, but I know that if I follow my path, the way will open and I will be led safely back to shore safe and sound.

Sometimes it can feel as if the tide has gone out and you are just drifting about in the water, but your spiritual path is your anchor and the tide will come in again and all will be well, all is well!

A lot of the time the answers to questions are within us. We just have to wait, listen and not distract ourselves by being busy. The answers often come in the silence of the heart. We have to get out of our own way and be led by the heart; the intellect is there to serve the wisdom of the heart.

Sometimes the answers come in dreams which we can, in turn, interpret, asking what the messages are. Answers may come in meditation, in the stillness and silence of the soul. Friends can sometimes point us in the right direction, but use your own discernment to find your answer. Look within - that is where you will find your answers. Listen to the messages from your body. Tune in and develop your intuition, listen to your gut feeling, be wise in your own judgement.

When the going gets tough, we are often in a rush for quick fix solutions such as medication, drugs or distractions. This is when your tool kit comes in - for example, EFT for uncomfortable emotions. Sometimes counselling is helpful, once the emotions present themselves.

Our thoughts can have a tendency to run off by themselves. It is quite useful to observe our thought pattern, as old negative patterns can keep us stuck in old ways; such negative feelings about ourselves can be the like of "I'm rubbish", when actually you may be very accomplished in some things. It is useful to keep a thought diary and observe how many times during the day you put yourself down.

Our thoughts are very powerful. If we alter our thoughts to more positive thoughts, we will attract positive things into our life. Thoughts can arise from our belief systems about ourselves and others. These are set in childhood, resulting from our environment and influences which occured whilst growing up. This, then affects our attitude to life and how we behave with ourselves and others.

Changing our belief systems is like turning a steam ship around. It is slow. It starts with increasing our awareness of our thought patterns and then altering our negative thoughts to more positive thoughts. Positive affirmations can be helpful when trying to do this and if you're feeling brave, look in the mirror as you are telling yourself how great you are.

Hatha yoga

Yoga is thousands of years old and consists of physical, mental and spiritual practices that help us to become more healthy and alert and, may even change our view of the world for the better.

The word yoga is Sanskrit, which is the ancient language of India, and means "union". Practising yoga helps to bring people together, bringing balance and harmony into our lives.

Benefits of practising yoga:

- Increases stamina and strength.
- Reduces tension and relaxes.
- Increases flexibility.
- Strengthens the immune system.
- Improves posture.
- Increases concentration.
- Prepares the body to sit in meditation.
- Helps us to feel into the body and listen to its messages.
- Memory is stored in the body, sometimes hidden from the conscious mind. Yoga helps us to uncover the memory.
- Helps us to heal from physical injury.

- Helps us to release emotional issues.
- Helps to energise the system.
- Helps us to feel more alive and optimistic.
- Creates a shift in the body which enables a shift in the mind.

Resistant comments

These are some of the comments that prevents people from gaining the benefits of yoga:

- "I'm not bendy" – It does not matter. Be happy where you are, there is no competition. Not even with yourself.
- "I have injuries" – A very good reason for practising gentle, restorative yoga. Find a teacher and a style that suits your body and temperament.
- "It is against my religious beliefs" - Yoga is universal and for everyone. It can be whatever you want it to be. It can be your spiritual path but it will not interfere with your own path.

Disadvantages to yoga

I cannot think of any. It's all good and a huge blessing for all of us, passed down through the wisdom of India throughout the centuries.

All we need to do is to get out of our own way, let the body be the conductor. Be totally present and allow the body to open and listen to the messages given by itself.
"Your Body Speaks your mind" by Debbie Shapiro(1996) helps to decipher the messages of the body and is a useful resource.

Nature
Painting, music and poetry

Painting is an expression of my deep love and gratitude for both animals and nature. Creativity came out of my "breakthrough", providing a balm for my soul and a way back to wholeness. Art is my outlet for the heart. I bare my soul in my paintings, painting a little bit of me each time. Painting is a meditation, showing me how I am feeling at a given time. Total concentration in the moment. I paint the animals with such love and feel a connection from heart to heart. I get to know each soul of the animal as I paint and each character is shown to me. They become part of me and I become part of them as I paint.

I paint scenery and become part of the landscape. I express my feelings through my painting. My connection to the land is set down for all to see, I am one with the land. I have included a selection of my poems and paintings within these pages.

Lifted straight from my spiritual diary, 2011:

Music stirs the depth of my soul, reaches my inner core, my inner cave, my cave of silence.

With intense emotion, I feel the violin and sense its language from anguish to lightness. The cello, ah! Melodic, grounding, reassuring, sturdy. The voice, a big black male bass voice like treacle; comforting, rich, deep molasses. The trumpet; joyous, light, mischievous, naughty.

Music
My Desert Island Disc List

1. Beethoven's *Symphony No. 9* – Tormented soul interspersed with beauty and deep love.
2. Rachmaninov's *Symphony No 2* – I can hardly reach the depths the music is wanting me to go it hurts my heart.
3. Philip Glass – *Concerto for Violin and Orchestra* Track 2 Reaches the depths so intense and all-consuming.
4. Johann Sebastian Bach - *Sheep May Safely Graze* - melodic calming joyous, nature at peace and at one .
5. Albinoni's *Adagio* – retreat, a balm for the soul.
6. *Schindlers List*- so so beautiful – poignant.
7. Johann Sebastian Bach - *Saint Matthew's Passion*- Bach with all his genius, a story is told of passion of pain. The cello, what can I say? The instrument that plays itself, the rousing chorus the blended voice, I energy, I connection, the sum of many parts, heavenly beings.
8. Karl Jenkins - *Stabat Mater – And my mother does weep*; Divine Mother's soul call to each and every one of us.
9. Bette Middler - *The Rose*. Being brave enough to open yourself to love and pain or miss out on all that life has to offer.

10. *Born Free* - Matt Monro - my beginning, middle and end, the lion and me born to be free. It's possible if we are courageous enough to take on the battle of life, let go and be free. We are all born to be free, the beautiful music stirs my childhood memory of my love for the lions and for the film. The resonance with the need for freedom.

Poetry

The Ocean

The vastness of the ocean a mirror of life within a continuum,
from calm to storm in an instant.
There is something mesmerising in the ebb and flow,
let it go it can't be controlled,
it has a life of its own a freedom without as freedom within.
It is without boundaries cannot be contained,
constant change always moving, always dancing,
indigo to turquoise all the colours under the sky;
what a dance what a life.

Black Hill Tree

An old gnarly tree
Stripped bare for all to see
Stark in its appearance
So barren and alone
THEN
Onto the canvas
A backdrop of colour
Splash on sharp azure
Brush on pale moor
Cushion the rustic ferns
To pay homage at thy feet

The old gnarly tree seems to have company
Several in a row
His part in creation solid and sure

And I have a portal into this scene
Spirit and nature dancing together
Through all the seasons and years
And in all kinds of weather
Not I on my own but we stand connected
Soul to soul as the artist intended

Camper van

Here I am again in my van
With not much idea of a plan
The weather is dreich
Which in English means bleak
YET
Today is a glory
On Easter Sunday
Jesus has risen indeed
And implanted in me his seed
The sun shines, the birds sing
Daffodils bloom the church bells ring
What a story there is to tell
Spring has sprung and all is well

The Solstice

The pause between the in breath and the out breath
Time stands still and All that is expands
The space within and the space without
Peace enfolds us, a welcome friend
Everything in rhythm, the ebb and the flow
The seasons come and go
Ancestors long gone and those yet to come
One in one out longest day shortest night
The cycle continues no beginning and no end
Just on and on and on and on

The Animals

The animals are my solace and my haven. They are my friends and my confidants. They offer me unconditional love. We, humans could learn a lot from our animal companions in trust, loyalty and being totally present in the moment. If only we could lose our ego and experience the divine love on offer.

I owe a huge debt of gratitude to my animal companions. Throughout my life they have been my shelter from the storm, a balm for my wounds and have walked by my side to a life of healing and wholeness. I would like to introduce you the reader to each beautiful soul one by one.

Snowy - my white cat in my childhood, constant and caring.

Tansot Timothy Trottwood - my longhaired Dachshund, given to me as a pup for my thirteenth birthday from Auntie Peggy. He was so kind, gentle and loyal, with big brown eyes. We had such fun together!

Mr. Pickwick - my horse as a teenager. With me from a foal to 5 years of age. What a character, plucky and obstinate with an indominitable spirit! I have had many dreams with us wandering the country lanes since we parted.

Jasper - jet black rescue cat who chose me, then also chose when to leave. Strong in character, independent in some ways but vulnerable in others. Physically weakened through life's battles. So sleek, so black and so male! Only with me for a short period, but left his indelible mark on me.

Carrot - my lovely ginger female cat, ever so shy, does not wander far, follows me about, ever-present, ever-chatting, she is magic. Her territory is round about, content to stay close, yet my lovely gentle friend can be feisty when she chooses to be.

Ruby - what can I say about my lovely Ruby red border Terrier companion? We wander for miles over the moors – she loves her moors, runs in circles, jumps for joy in tipply top tails, round and round in circles, with such zest for life and in the moment of sheer pleasure. However, if she does not want to go in a certain direction, then she will not budge. What a mind of her own, what willpower, what stubbornness! Her face tells you everything. Ruby and I have been on a journey; she has taught me such a lot about dogs, both emotionally and physically. Ruby has turned everything I knew about dogs upside down. I owe her huge gratitude for her teaching, love, friendship, loyalty. Ruby is my best friend, my constant companion. We are devoted to each other. What a blessing to have her in my life!

My Best Friends

Meander Meander Meander
Where am I going
Where have I been
I walk alone talk alone
Connect with Masters unseen
Alone Alone Alone Alone
But for my companions
Present and unconditional
A love so deep it calls for me to weep
Animals and me dancing together
Forever Forever Forever Forever

Horses as Healers and Teachers

"My Journey in the saddle back to the Heart"

For the last three years, I have made my way back to horses, back to my childhood, with the support and guidance of my friend Helen. Only, the connection with horses is now on a totally different level and I believe it is because of my ability, through meditation practice, to create a quiet space within. I am more able to get out of my own way. It is in the peace that a deep connection with the horse occurs.

They feel and understand how we are inside, often better than we do ourselves. They are preyed-upon animals, so it is in their interest as a matter of survival to sense a perceived threat. They can also assist us in making a shift on how we feel inside and help us on our healing journey. This process is explained really well in The "Listening Heart" by Leigh Shambo (2013) and also in Linda Korhanov's books the "Tao of Equus" (2007) and "Riding Between the Worlds"(2007).

For me, the experience of deep healing and connection preceded the reading in any book and I struggle to articulate what happened between the horses and myself, different horses, different experiences at different times. I have not the words to explain it. Everyone needs to find the experience for themselves, which occurs when the person is ready. It isn't about doing, expecting anything or even touching.

The horse has a precious gift to offer, but only when we are ready to receive it. We cannot force it! We need to prepare ourselves and our inner world. Using the methods in this book may help in this preparation along with meditation, which is the key to unblocking the mystery.

In the book "One with the Herd"(2007), Liz Mitten Ryan talks about spending time with her herd of horses and being accepted into their world with quietness, patience and having a sense of belonging. They become a mirror of how we really feel inside ourselves and within our community, even if we are not fully aware.

Mark Rashid, in his book "The Heart of Passive Leadership"(2011), talks about the way horses interact in the herd and discusses some of the methods he uses when working with horses, different ways at different times. I came away with the message that whatever method is used with horses and however "natural" it seems to be, no method can be the right one when there is an ingredient missing. This missing ingredient is often LOVE. If we don't come from a place of love, then no method, however natural, can be the right one.

My friend, Helen Brennand, who introduced me to this new world with the horses has written a beautiful book entitled "Belief". She talks about her connection to her horses and the deep love they exchange, written in poetic language with the depth and feeling expressed from her soul.

I would like to introduce you to Helen's horses:

Remedy (chestnut warm blood)
When tests have been passed and veils removed, in comes

proud, majestic, courageous Remedy, a beautiful chestnut mare, all-knowing, gentle and firm like a reverend mother, helping me to discover my childhood dreams and longings that do not go away. They just remain dormant like hidden treasures, re-emerging when the time is right and oh, what treasures! It's well worth waiting for.

We helped each other to heal our wounds. She knows because she has been there. Remedy reaches a deep place within my heart and soul and we emerge together into the light.

This would not have been possible without Matthew Brennand's generosity of spirit in allowing me to spend time with his horse companion. I will always be grateful for this. It is an example of how we all have a part to play in the weaving of the web. This book was finally born after my deep healing with the horses had cleared the way.

Cookie (A bay pony)

What can I say? A survivor, a character, a sensitive soul. He makes me laugh. We are paving out our path and purpose in life of usefulness together. We mirror each other and learn from each other and help each other to reset our neural pathways. Be warned - Cookie will test your patience. This is your lesson but he will also help you to love yourself.

Revel (A bay pony)

Revel offers unconditional love from heart to heart. She is a wise old soul - gentle, but don't be misled! She is feisty and all-knowing and sees through any veneer, straight to the heart. With Revel, we get a taste of our connection to Divine

Mother, who is waiting for us here and now, once we get out of our own way. Revel reminds us that each and every one of us is really really loved just as we are. Revel shows us a glimpse of this.

Billy (A coloured pony)

He is so grounded! Solid as a rock, stubborn at times and an open book. What a great teacher he is - he knows exactly what's going on. If you do not concentrate, focus and connect with him in the moment, then forget it. He will not budge or take a hike because he is teaching his lessons, teaching me how to up my game and my energy and how to be a leader; assertive, but not aggressive and, what a great teacher he is! Playing his part, he is so relaxed and so happy, especially in the fields with his lady friends: Remedy and Donner. He also has a wonderful companionship with Emma, his special human friend.

Donner (A Bay warm blood)

Last, but by no means least, Donner is the leader of her herd and is pure love and joy. A testament to Helen's careful handling, because she is always tuned in to Donner's mood and her needs and their mutual love and friendship is plain to see. They dance together in pure harmony.

Untouched by human ego, power, mislead dominance or harsh handling. This is how it should and will be when the veils are removed and we all come from love. The love, friendship and respect between Donner and Helen shines through. They are equal partners. Donner is not a push-over. She is the leader of the herd, but Helen is up to her position through love, assertiveness, clear boundaries and awareness of safety. They are both present and aware. What a team they make!

We start with loving ourselves then we give that love to all. That is all there is when the kernel is polished and the love shines through. All the animals play their part once we are open to it.

And the Doves of peace arrive, love peace and joy in "THE HAVEN" (www.Belief444.com)

Life

We erupt from the womb as a kernel revealed
The drama begins of mystery, of thriller, of joy, its a killer
Time marches on the kernel is cloaked, the crustaceans rock
hard
Layer on layer the scene is set, a dormant time unloved and
cloaked
Tick tock, tick tock, tick tock, tick tock

Then all of a sudden opportunity knocks the peeling begins
Release release polish and clean, emerge from the gloom
As the wine matures and begins to pour
The kernel is polished as never before
The blinkers are off and all is clear
Awaken awaken and live your dreams
Your time has come there is work to be done
A jewel in the crown and a pure white gown
As we turn the page and we ripen with age
Our goals are achieved, it's hard to believe
Now its time to wander back home to our ready made tomb

We have done our best, and arrive in bliss, and now it's our
time for a well deserved rest

Conclusion

So there you have it. We have a choice. We can remain stuck, feeling sorry for ourselves and going round the same circles and patterns, or we can choose to get off the merry go round and develop new ways, remove the veils, see the light and step into freedom.

We have the tools to achieve this at our fingertips. We just have to use them. The time is right, we now have a portal into the higher realms and a chance to clear. We are fully supported and never truly alone.

If we can recognise the ancestral patterns that have kept us stuck in old ways, undo them by finding a new way of reacting to them, not only do we help to heal ourselves, but also past and future generations benefit, by observing a healthier approach to life. We are their role model and we can present a new way of living. We can also learn from the young ones who still have a blank sheet without the conditioning.

Our life is our responsibility. We have chosen this life

for the lessons necessary for our growth. We cannot blame others or blame the situation, or absolve responsibility for our lot onto another. We need to change the tape and look for opportunities and signs to keep moving, ever onward and upward. Our karma is our karma and, out of our suffering, new seeds are sown, new openings and a new future await us - if that is what we would like - but we have to do the work required.

The time is right to shift the veils, wake up and grasp your life and everything that is on offer to you. Darkness is to be brought into the light. My next book would be aptly named "Surviving to Thriving"!

We have the books, teachers, tools and wisdom of the ages. All you need is the courage to take it and follow the path laid out for you. There is only love and fear. Fear keeps us trapped, whereby love gives us freedom. What path are you going to choose for yourself? I know what I am choosing for myself.

Once you have found your light, it is then time to shine brightly. Don't diminish your light because others cannot cope or are not ready to find their own. Remember, your path is your path. As Mahatma Ghandi said:

"Be the change you want to see in the world"

Good luck on the journey they call life and do not forget to take your sense of humour with you. Let's face it, we all need one!

Love,
Janice

Further reading

Below is a list of books that have helped me, it is not an exhaustive list just some that I have chosen.

Chodron, P., (2005). *When Things Falls Apart,* Third Edition. London: Harper Collins.
Coelho, P., (1993). *The Alchemist.* First English Edition. London: Harper Collins.
Chopra, D., (2001). *Perfect Health.* Third Edition. London: Bantum Books.
Edwards, B., (1993). *Drawing on the Right Side of the Brain.* Revised Edition. UK: Harper Collins.
Hey, L., (1984). *You Can Heal Your Life.* UK: Hay House.
Peck, S., (1999). *The Road Less Travelled and Beyond.* Second Edition. London: Rider.
Redfield, J., (2000). *Secret of Shambala.* Second Edition. London: Bantum Books.
Villoldo, A. Phd., (2005). *Mending the Past and Healing the Future with Soul Retrieval.* First Edition. UK: Hay House.
Yogananda, P., (2000). *The Autobiography of a Yogi.* USA: Self Realization Fellowship.

Websites:
Vibro Harmonization Technique: www.vhtworld.com. Developed by Jock Ruddock.
HEA Training Programme, The Prevention and Management of Stress, Health. Skills Project, Counselling and Career Development Unit, Uni-

versity of Leeds.

Nurick, Dr. R., Johnson, Dr. V., Development Focus UK, Regeneration Through Community Appraisal, Trainees and Training Programme. www.developmentfocus.org.uk.

The White Eagle Publishing Trust - www.whiteeaglepublishing.org, Hampshire, England.

Craig, G. - *EFT - www.emofree.com*

Bibliography/References

Bays, B., (1999). *The Journey. First Edition. Australia: Atria Harper Collins.*

Brennand, H., (2014). *Belief.* UK: Creative Locations Ltd.

Byrne, R., (2006). *The Secret.* Atria: Australia, Canada, United Kingdom.

Craig, G., (2008). *EFT Manual.* UK: Energy Psychology Press.

D'Adamo, Dr. P, J., (1996). *Eat Right For Your Type.* New York: G P Putnam's and Sons.

Harnish, C. L., (2007). *Path of the Soul Destiny Cards. UK: Spirits Way Designs.*

Hicks, J., Hicks, E., (2010). *Ask And It Is Given.* Second Edition. UK: Hay House.

Holford, P., (2008). *Optimum Nutrition Made Easy. Second Edition. London: Piatkus Books.*

Kohanov, L., (2007). *The Tao Of Equus, First Edition. California: New World Library.*

Kohanov, L., (2007). *Riding Between The Worlds. First Edition. California: New World Library.*

Plotkin, B., (2003). *Soulcraft. First Edition. California: New World Library.*

Peck, S., (1990). People of The Lie. Second Edition. London: Arrow.

Rashid, M., (2011). Horses Never Lie The Heart Of Passive Leadership. Second Edition. Devon: Skyhorse Publishing.

Ryan, L. M., (2007). One with the Herd. First Edition. New Hampshire: Liz Mitten Ryan.

Shambo, L., (2013). The Listening Heart. First Edition. USA: Human Equine Alliance for Learning.

Shapiro, D., (2008). Your Body Speaks Your Mind. Fourth Edition. London: Piatkus Books

Tolle, E., (1999). The Power of Now. First Edition. USA: New World Library.

Williamson, M., (1996). A Return to Love. Second Edition. London: Harper Collins.

Villoldo, A., (2012). Courageous Dreaming. Fourth Edition. UK: Hay House.

Yogananda, P., (2003). Living Fearlessly. First Edition. California: Self-Realization Fellowship.

"When I am gone, only love can take my place."
Paramahansa Yogananda